W

A Guide to the Most Common Whiskeys, and How to Know the Difference between the Good, Bad and the Ugly

Table of Contents

Thank you! _____ 3

Introduction _____ 6

Chapter 1 – Whiskey 101 _____ 7

Chapter 2 – Why Do People Drink Whiskey? _____ 13

Chapter 3 – History of Whiskey _____ 17

Chapter 4 – Things You May Not Know About Whiskey ___ 21

Chapter 5 – How to Tell if a Bottle of Whiskey is Fake ____ 30

Chapter 6 – Whiskey Cocktail Recipes _____ 33

Conclusion _____ 38

Check Out My Other Books _____ 40

Greetings from the Lean Stone Publishing Company ____ 42

Thank you!

Thank you for buying this book!

If you enjoy the book and get some value from it, I would appreciate if you could **leave an honest review** on the Amazon store after finishing.

Thank you and enjoy the book!

***

Receive updates on new book releases, book promotions and much more from Tadio Diller by signing up to the e-mail list: **http://bit.ly/list_tadiodiller_cs**

***

Follow us, Lean Stone Publishing, the publishing company that published this book. You will receive information on upcoming book launches, free book promotions and much more. Sign up to this e-mail list: **http://bit.ly/list_lsp_cs**

***

Like us at **www.facebook.com/leanstonepublishing**

Follow us on Twitter **@leanstonebooks**

©**Copyright 2015 by Tadio Diller - All rights reserved.**

This document is geared towards providing exact and reliable information in regards to the topic and issue covered. The publication is sold with the idea that the publisher is not required to render accounting, officially permitted, or otherwise, qualified services. If advice is necessary, legal or professional, a practiced individual in the profession should be ordered.

- From a Declaration of Principles which was accepted and approved equally by a Committee of the American Bar Association and a Committee of Publishers and Associations.

In no way is it legal to reproduce, duplicate, or transmit any part of this document in either electronic means or in printed format. Recording of this publication is strictly prohibited and any storage of this document is not allowed unless with written permission from the publisher. All rights reserved.

The information provided herein is stated to be truthful and consistent, in that any liability, in terms of inattention or otherwise, by any usage or abuse of any policies, processes, or directions contained within is the solitary and utter responsibility of the recipient reader. Under no circumstances will any legal responsibility or blame be held against the publisher for any reparation, damages, or monetary loss due to the information herein, either directly or indirectly.

Respective authors own all copyrights not held by the publisher.

The information herein is offered for informational purposes solely, and is universal as so. The presentation of the information is without contract or any type of guarantee assurance.

The trademarks that are used are without any consent, and the publication of the trademark is without permission or backing by the trademark owner. All trademarks and brands within this book are for clarifying purposes only and are the owned by the owners themselves, not affiliated with this document.

Introduction

I want to thank you and congratulate you for buying the book, *"Whiskey: A Guide to the Most Common Whiskeys, and How to Know the Difference between the Good, Bad and the Ugly"*

This book contains information about whiskey, including its history, the different types, and how to better appreciate the drink. Also included in this book are other bits of info, like tips on how to identify fake whiskeys, and also a couple of cocktail recipes involving whiskey, in case you want to try something new.

Why is whiskey so appealing? This "real man's drink" has been one of the most popular drinks to ever grace the earth, and yet it can be the most intimidating drink for the uninitiated. First off, there are many different kinds of whiskey to choose from, that just the sheer number of them usually puts off aspiring enthusiasts. There is also the storing and serving aspect with regards to being a whiskey connoisseur. You also need to learn about the equipment needed, and the proper ways to serve whiskey.

In this book, all possible questions regarding whiskey will be answered, so budding whiskey enthusiasts, such as yourself, will have no trouble easing into your new hobby. You will learn everything every beginner needs to know, like the history of whiskey, how to distinguish the different types from one another, and how to serve whiskey in different ways. By the end of this book, you will know so much about whiskey, that it will only make you want to learn more, which is not necessarily a bad thing.

Thanks again for downloading this book, I hope you enjoy it!

Chapter 1 – Whiskey 101

Long since considered a "real man's drink", whiskey is now crossing the gender borders as many women are taking an interest in this alcoholic beverage. However, what is it about whiskey that makes it one of the most enduring liquors the world has ever seen?

Etymology

The first thing that you need to know is where it got its name. How did the word "whiskey" (sometimes spelled as whisky) come about? Historians say that the word *whiskey* is the Anglicization of the Gaelic word, *uisce* or *uisge*, which was in turn derived from the Latin term used to describe any alcoholic drink, *aqua vitae (water of life)*; *uisce beatha* in Gaelic. Other early English spellings of whiskey include *iskie bae* (from the 1580s) and *usquebea* (from 1706).

Whiskey or Whisky?

You may have noticed, while browsing the liquor aisle of your local grocery, that there are two distinct spellings for this alcoholic drink: *whiskey* and *whisky*. Although it may seem like a trivial matter, serious whiskey enthusiasts will likely berate you if you ever mixed up these terms; they strongly believe that these are not just two different spellings of the same word. According to them, if the liquor came from the United States or Ireland, then it is *whiskey*, but if its country of origin is Canada, Scotland, or (strangely enough) Japan, then it is *whisky*.

You might think that this is not really that big of a deal, but you must not underestimate the passion of whiskey/whisky drinkers. Once in 2008, a columnist from the prestigious New York Times ignored this spelling rule (or they may have been completely ignorant of it), and used the term *whiskey* all the time, regardless of where the liquor came from, which ruffled quite a lot of feathers in the whiskey/whisky world.

After receiving a deluge of complaints, some even came from within the columnist's own social circle, he made a public apology (sort of), and he said that he never claimed to be an expert in whiskey/y and he never meant to "offend" people by his choice of words.

Now, if you do not want to find yourself in the same predicament as the hapless New York Times columnist, here is a quick rule of thumb: if the country of origin has an "e" in its name (Unit*E*d Stat*E*s, Ir*E*land) then it is *whiskey*; if it does not (Canada, Japan, Scotland) then it is *whisky*.

However, for convenience, this book will henceforth just use the term "whiskey" to prevent confusing the reader.

What is Whiskey?

Enough about the etymology of whiskey, it is time for you to actually learn a bit about the drink itself. First, what is it that makes whiskey different from other kinds of liquor?

Whiskey pertains to any kind of liquor distilled from a grain mash; however, you can exempt bourbon from that rule because it contains mostly corn. Another thing, the distilled liquor must be at least 40% alcohol by volume (ABV), which is to say, it must be strong enough to make you grow hair on your chest.

To put it in even simpler terms, whiskey is just distilled beer. Malted barley, sometimes combined with other grains, are steeped in hot water to release the natural sugars in them. The resulting liquid, known as the "wort", is then cooled down, and then yeast is added to kick-start the fermentation process, the end result of which is beer.

However, the beer created for whiskey making purposes (otherwise called the 'wash') will not contain hops. Beer makers introduce hops to the wash to balance out their natural sweetness, which is why beer has that distinct, bitter flavor. Whiskey distillers, on the other hand, take the wash, distill it to increase the alcohol content, and then age it in oak barrels to balance out the sweetness.

The Different Kinds of Whiskey

Just like the other kinds of spirits, there are also different types of whiskey, and they are classified according to the grains used in production, and the area where they are made. Although there are dozens of types of whiskey, this book will concentrate only on the most popular types, which are Scotch, Bourbon, Rye, and Irish whiskey.

Scotch

As the name implies, Scotch whiskey must come from Scotland. Any country can copy the recipes and methods of making Scotch whiskey, but unless it actually came from Scotland, it is technically still ordinary whiskey.

Besides the location, Scotch whiskey must use mostly malted barley as an ingredient, although you can use other grains to add flavor and color to the product. Besides yeast, you must never use any other fermentation additive to make Scotch; in fact, some distillers use only three ingredients when making whiskey: malted barley, yeast, and water.

Finally, Scotch must be aged in oak barrels for no less than 3 years, and it should at least have 94.8% alcohol content.

Bourbon

Just like Scotch, whiskey can only claim the distinction of being called Bourbon if it was made in the United States. Besides the location, bourbon whiskey must be made from a mash that contains no less than 51% corn. In most cases, distillers do not use fresh yeast every time they make a batch of bourbon. They would usually just add some of the fermenting mash from a previous batch to the new one; this process is known as sour mash.

It is also important to note that for a whiskey to get the label of bourbon, the requirement is that it must be no less than 62.5% ABV, and no more than 80% before placing them in charred oak barrels for aging. Although there are no strict aging requirements for bourbon, to be classified as 'straight bourbon', it must be aged in oak barrels for no less than two years.

Rye Whiskey

Rye whiskey is a bit trickier to explain, and it all stemmed from the historical naming convention regarding the rye whiskey produced in Canada. The tricky part is that most people would assume that rye whiskey must be made entirely of rye mash, which seems obvious, but most people would be wrong on that account.

Canadians have been distilling rye whiskey ever since Canada came into existence; however, since the rules regarding the making of rye whiskey have not been firmly established, unlike Scotch and bourbon, the ingredients and processes involved in making 'true' rye whiskey are a bit blurry. Some makers even use a 9:1 corn mash to make a rye mash mixture, which would technically make it bourbon. The only rules that are currently in place for a whiskey to gain the Canadian rye whiskey label are that it must contain at least some rye.

American rye whiskey, on the other hand, must be made from a mash that is at least 51% rye, and follows the same alcohol content and aging rules as bourbon.

Irish Whiskey

Just like Scotch whiskey, Irish whiskey must be made entirely in Ireland, obviously. However, that is where the similarities end. Just like Canadian rye whiskey, Irish whiskeys have very relaxed rules when it comes to their labeling, their rules are actually more relaxed. There are no set rules on what grains to use for making Irish whiskey, which is why it has the most diverse array of choices among all whiskey types.

Subtypes of Whiskey

Besides the country of origin, there are three sub-types of whiskey, depending on how they are bottled and sold: the single malt, single cask, and blended.

Single malt whiskey is the most common type that you will find in the market these days. These spirits come from combining whiskey that came from the same distillery, and most of the time using the same recipe. The age of the youngest batch of whiskey put into the mix will be the age of the bottled product.

Single cask whiskey is a bit rarer than single malt. Unlike single malt whiskey, the contents of a single cask whiskey bottle came from just one cask or barrel; there is no mixing involved. Because these types of whiskeys usually come from small, independent distilleries, and by the larger companies in very limited amounts, single cask whiskeys can be extremely expensive.

Blended whiskeys, as the name suggests, are a mix of whiskeys of the same type, but they come from different distilleries. Some bottlers do blend different types of whiskey, like scotch and bourbon, but they are extremely rare. Most whiskey experts scoff at the thought of blended whiskey, and most of their tirades are somewhat valid. However, there are companies, like Johnny Walker, that only sell blended whiskey, that are quite popular with whiskey lovers.

These are just some of the many types of whiskeys available. If you truly want to become a serious enthusiast, then you should check out the other kinds from different countries. At the start, you might think that all whiskeys taste the same, but after some time, and tasting a few more types, you will realize that there are humongous flavor differences between them.

Chapter 2 – Why Do People Drink Whiskey?

Some people may be perplexed as to why whiskey lovers actually like drinking whiskey, and they are somewhat right to wonder. Whiskey enthusiasts certainly do not drink whiskey just for the sake of getting drunk - that would be a very expensive way to get buzzed. The extremely high alcohol content also means that most people who love whiskey did not start drinking it because it tasted great; in fact, it will burn your taste buds if you take it straight for the first time. So, why do many people enjoy whiskey so much that it became such a gigantic industry?

An Acquired Taste

To say that whiskey is an acquired taste is an understatement. For the uninitiated, drinking straight whiskey can be an excruciating experience; the extremely high alcohol content means it will be a bit rough going down, and in most cases, it will make you gag. First timers will often find it hard to distinguish between all of the different tastes that whiskey lovers describe enthusiastically; the smoke flavor reminiscent of campfires, the wood flavor that came from the oak barrels they were aged in, and others too.

Not being able to identify this wondrous world of flavors the first time is usually enough to discourage most aspiring whiskey connoisseurs, but they really should not let their first time dictate whether or not they like whiskey.

Alcohol Content and Why It Matters

If this is your first time trying whiskey, then you might want to check the alcohol content first before you even buy a bottle. It has been mentioned numerous times already that whiskey is notorious for having a high alcohol content, and if you are not careful, your first experience with whiskey will not be all that pleasant.

Understanding the Proof

While most whiskeys have the alcohol content printed right on their labels, albeit they are usually in the fine print on the back, but one thing is for sure, they will have the 'proof' in bold letters on the front of the bottle. However, it can be confusing, because the number of the proof is not equivalent to the actual alcohol content of the whiskey.

Simply put, the number of the proof is twice the actual alcohol content of the whiskey; therefore, if you see a bottle that says it is 120 proof, then it has 60 percent alcohol by volume (ABV). If you are a beginner in the whiskey tasting world, then you should probably start with high quality, 80-proof whiskey (40% ABV is the absolute minimum for whiskeys); this still might seem a bit too strong, but it is manageable.

Scrutinizing Your Whiskey

Most people would think that only the sense of taste matters when it comes to appreciating whiskey and other alcoholic beverages, but the truth is that you need to engage all of your senses when drinking it.

Look at the Whiskey

Before you drink your whiskey, you need to do a simple visual scrutiny first. Take the time to look at the color and clarity of the whiskey you have in your glass. Generally, the older the whiskey, the darker its color because it was exposed longer to the charred wooden barrels. For instance, a whiskey left to age in a barrel for 2 years will have a straw-like color, while an older variant left to age for a couple of years more may have the same golden brown color of a freshly-made pretzel.

Take note though that some of the cheaper brands of whiskey will use artificial means to give their products a deeper color, so be wary of bottles that say that they contain 2-year old whiskey, but have a dark khaki color to it.

Smell the Whiskey

Unlike wine makers, whiskey distillers rely more on their noses rather than their tongues when checking their wares. You may not know this, but your nose can actually tell you what a particular food will taste like before it even touches your tongue, which is why it is somewhat hard to taste food when you have a cold.

When smelling your whiskey, you should not thrust your nose straight into your glass, since if you do, the alcohol will most likely overwhelm your sense of smell. The proper way is to slowly raise your glass to your nose, and swirl the contents a bit before taking a whiff. Take note of all the things you smell because it will be indicative of what the whiskey will actually taste like. If you get a hint of smoke then you will most likely taste it when you take a sip.

Tasting the Whiskey

Okay, you have held yourself back long enough, it is time for you to taste the whiskey. However, do not just chug the entire contents of your glass in one gulp; you are here to appreciate the whiskey, not get drunk. Take a sip of the alcohol, but before you swallow, make sure that you coat your tongue evenly with whiskey, and let the liquid stay on your palate for a bit.

How does the whiskey feel in your mouth? Does it feel thin, or is it a bit viscous? What flavor notes do you notice? Do you taste the smokiness from the oak barrels? Do you sense that slight flavor of port wine? How long did the flavor of the whiskey linger in your mouth after swallowing? Now, ask yourself, did you enjoy that first sip?

If you feel like your choice of whiskey is a bit too overpowering, then you can splash a bit of water in your glass to cut down the alcohol content. Doing this will also release most of the whiskey's aromas and flavors, making it even easier for you to enjoy your drink.

As you can see, whiskey tasting is a treat for almost all of your senses. Your first glass of whiskey may not seem that enjoyable, but give yourself a bit of time. Let your taste buds mature a bit and soon you will learn to like, if not love, the complexity and exquisite flavor of whiskey.

Chapter 3 – History of Whiskey

Whiskey has been around for hundreds of years, and its history is almost as vibrant as its taste. Now, you might be thinking to yourself, "why am I getting a history lesson now, aren't I just supposed to learn about whiskey?" Although it is not a requirement that you know the complete history of whiskey to become a connoisseur, knowing where it came from and how it evolved to become one of the most popular drinks in the world does actually make you appreciate it more.

The Distillation Process

Before we head out to the origins of whiskey, we must first discuss the discovery of the distillation process. Archaeological records suggest that the ancient Babylonians were the first ones to use the distillation process; however, they most likely used it to create perfumes. There are also historical records that tell about how the ancient Greeks could have also used distillation, but again, they did not use them for making booze. In fact, they did not even use it for alcohol production. Even so, the methods of distillation have been passed down from one ancient civilization to the next.

Whiskey in the Middle Ages

It was not until the 13th century in Italy when distillation was actually used to produce alcohol, when monks distilled alcohol from wine, but since the end product was extremely unpalatable, it was mostly used for medicinal purposes. Arnald of Villanova, a doctor and teacher at one of the first medical schools in Europe, hand-wrote the concise instructions for distilling alcohol, calling it *aqua vitae*, which is 'water of life' in Latin.

Although *aqua vitae* was originally meant to be used as medicine, that changed once they made their way into Ireland and Scotland. The Irish and the Scots are actually still at odds as to who actually made whiskey first. The Irish say that whisky came from the Emerald Isles; according to the Annals of Clonmacnoise, there was an entry about the death of a chieftain due to "taking a surfeit of *aqua vitae*" during Christmas celebrations.

The Scots, however, claim that whiskey started with them. There is an entry in the Exchequer Rolls, wherein a certain Friar Cor received a shipment of malt to make 500 bottles of *aqua vitae* by the order of the king. Whoever it was who first made whiskey, one thing is for sure, we have them to thank for giving the modern world this heavenly drink.

In 1725, almost all of Scotland's distillation operations were either shut down, or forced to hide and go underground because of the excessive English Malt Tax. Back in those days, the Scots were forced to hide their whiskey everywhere; they hid it in coffins, under the pulpit of churches, and other places just so they could avoid the English tax collectors.

In fact, it was estimated that at that time, almost fifty percent of all the whiskey in Scotland was manufactured illegally. Distillers back then used homemade stills and resorted to making their products during the night, so that the English authorities would not see the smoke coming out of their equipment, and this is why bootleg liquor is now called "moonshine".

Coming to America

Although whiskey came into the United States much later than the rest of the Western world, it still had a deep impact on the country's history.

The Whiskey Rebellion

One of the most famous events in US history, which had anything to do with whiskey, is the aptly named the Whiskey Rebellion. It happened during the first couple of years of George Washington's presidency. In order to devise a way for the Federal Government to pay its outstanding national debt, they imposed a tax on alcoholic spirits, and since whiskey was the most popular one at the time, the people called this new government excise the "whiskey tax".

Naturally, the people were outraged about this new tax, which they believed was a classic example of the very thing they fought against during the Revolutionary War, which was taxation without representation. Farmers resisted this new tax because they would usually brew and distill their grain surplus to prevent them from spoiling, and they would usually just make whiskey for their own consumption.

Although the Whiskey Rebellion was mostly non-violent, the whiskey tax proved to be very difficult to collect, and it seemed that the Federal Government was spending more money than it is collecting. However, Washington continued enforcing this tax as a demonstration of how his government had the political will and ability to enforce the laws. It was not until Thomas Jefferson took over the reins of government that the whiskey tax was repealed.

During Prohibition

The US Senate approved the 18th Amendment to the Constitution in 1919. This act aimed at making the production and sale of alcoholic beverages illegal, (unless it is used for religious purposes, mostly the wine used in Catholic mass). This amendment was more popularly known as the Prohibition. Although the motives of the government for approving the enforcement of the Prohibition laws were somewhat noble, it hurt the country more than actually helping; and the whiskey distillers received the brunt of the blow.

Since the production of whiskey was outlawed, it forced most of the distillers to go underground, or for the sake of survival, they started making other products. This led to extensive bootlegging and hoarding operations, and since there are no government agencies that monitored the quality of the whiskey that went into the black market, it was actually a risky time to become a whiskey connoisseur.

Some whiskey manufacturers actually found a loophole in the system during Prohibition; they could market their wares as medical whiskey. At the time, people still believed that whiskey had medicinal properties (it was called *aqua vitae*, after all), but people could only get it with a prescription. People were allowed a pint of whiskey every ten days, which was a small amount, but beggars cannot be choosers. If they wanted whiskey that was safe to drink, then they had to speak with their doctors.

Post Prohibition and During World War II

On December 5, 1933, exactly fourteen years, five months, and four days after its enactment, the 18th Amendment to the United States Constitution, also known as the Prohibition, was repealed. On that day, the production of whiskey and other alcoholic beverages was once again legal, which was really good news for the struggling distilling industries.

However, the reunion of the American drinking public and whiskey was short-lived. A few short years after the repulsion of the Prohibition, the looming war against Nazi Germany forced the government to go into self-preservation mode; thus, suspending the production of non-essential items, such as whiskey, and concentrating most of the workforce to the war effort.

Chapter 4 – Things You May Not Know About Whiskey

Besides knowing the history of the world's most famous spirit, it will also be beneficial if you know a bit of trivia about whiskey. Although knowing these things may not enhance your drinking experience much, they will; however, make you a better conversationalist, which is always a good quality in a drinking buddy.

A Safe Killed Jack Daniels

Probably one of the most well-known American whiskey manufacturers, Jack Daniels, actually died in a not-so-classy manner. It all began one morning when Daniels tried repeatedly to open the safe in his office. Frustrated that he could not get the safe to open, Daniels kicked it so hard that he broke his toe. Unfortunately, his toe never healed, and because medical science was still not up to snuff back then, the broken toe got infected and festered, resulting to Jack Daniels' death in 1911.

1. *Whiskey is heavily taxed in the United States.* Do you still remember the *whiskey tax* discussed in an earlier chapter? Apparently, it is still enforced up to this day, albeit going under another name. Whiskey is one of the most taxed commodities in the US; in fact, almost half of whiskey's selling price goes directly to taxes.

2. *Glass prevents the whiskey from aging any further.* Aging refers to the time the whiskey spent inside oak barrels prior to bottling. So even if you have a bottle of whiskey from the 1970s, its age is still the one written on its label.

3. *Angels steal your whiskey.* For every year that whiskey spends in a barrel, 4% of its volume is lost due to evaporation; distillers call this the "angel's tax". However, once the whiskey is bottled, the "angels" cannot get a hold of it anymore.

4. *The "angel's tax" helps increase the value of a particular batch of whiskey.* Since 4% of the total volume of whiskey is lost every year it is aged in barrels, it also means that there is less of the product after it finishes aging, and this drives up the price of the contents.

5. *Speaking of aging, most whiskeys will not improve in taste after passing the 25-year mark.* If you see a bottle of whiskey aged 30 to 40 years, it may only be rarer, but will not taste any different from a 20 or 25-year old whiskey.

6. *Some people are genetically predisposed not to like the taste of whiskey.* Just as some people find the taste of cilantro disgusting (some people have this particular gene in them that makes them taste cilantro as 'soapy'), some people also find the taste of certain scotch whiskeys disgusting. Although it is yet to be confirmed, some say that whiskeys, to them, taste like 'burnt ass'.

7. *The most expensive bottle of whiskey sold for more than $600,000.00.* A large decanter of Macallan "M" whiskey is probably the most expensive bottle of whiskey ever; it went for $628,205 in a high-end auction in Hong Kong, to a very wealthy Chinese businessman. What was so special about this particular bottle of spirits, you ask? For one thing, only four bottles were ever made, and secondly, the resident

whiskey maker/blender of Macallan spent two years searching for the 7 casks (out of the 200,000 in their inventory) to make the final product.

8. *Your freezer is not cold enough to turn whiskey into ice.* Whiskey can withstand temperatures ranging from -20 to -30 degrees, so your average domestic freezer will not be powerful enough to freeze even a cheap bottle of whiskey. However, it is not really recommended that you chill the drink.

9. *President Lyndon B. Johnson's favorite drink of all time was Jack and Coke.* He would often ride around his Texas property in an open top convertible, with a plastic foam cup of the cocktail in hand. Whenever his cup was empty, he would just dangle it out on the side of the car and the Secret Service would refill it for him.

10. *Whiskey makers and dairy farmers work hand-in-hand.* Dairy farmers just adore whiskey makers, not just because of the heavenly liquid that goes out their doors, but also because of what they discard. The grain mash left over from the whiskey making process is full of vitamins and nutrients, and cows seem to love them too. This means that whiskey makers do not need to pay someone to dispose of their production waste, and dairy farmers get free feed for their livestock. It is a win-win situation for both parties.

11. *The French love whiskey more than their own cognac.* The French love Scotch whiskey so much that there are more bottles of it sold per month than cognac per year. Even though Americans import around 120 million bottles of Scotch per year, it does not even come close to

the 200 million bottles that the French import on an annual basis.
12. *Irish whiskey is a lot smoother than other whiskey types because it is distilled three times.* Triple distillation means that the Irish take out most, if not all, of the impurities in their whiskey, making it easier to drink, and easier to get carried away, so be wary of how much of the stuff you drink.

13. *An unopened bottle of whiskey can be stored for more than a hundred years, and it will still be okay to drink; however, an opened bottle of whiskey will only last five years tops.* Once you open a bottle of whiskey, its flavor will immediately start to deteriorate, and once it reaches the five-year mark, it will be just a shadow of its former self. However, true whiskey connoisseurs will not wait that long to finish just one bottle.

14. *During their expeditions, Lewis and Clarke would ration their men with one cup of whiskey each.* Some men would actually horde their daily allowance of whiskey until they had enough to get themselves black out drunk. To prevent this from happening, Lewis and Clarke would have the men drink the whiskey in front of them, and make them stick out their tongues to prove that they actually swallowed their drink. The reason they did this is because a single drunk person on their expedition may have jeopardized the lives of the rest.

15. *The Brits export more whiskey than they keep.* The British are more willing to give out their whiskey to the rest of the world rather than sell them to local bar patrons.

16. *Scotland almost has the monopoly when it comes to whisky.* It is estimated that almost 90 percent of all the single malt whiskey in the world right now hailed from Scotland.

17. *Mountain Dew was originally meant to be a chaser for whiskey.* The original makers of Mountain Dew, brothers Barney and Ally Hartman, were looking for a good chaser to make whiskey a bit more amicable to their stomachs, but their search was futile, so they decided to make their own. It is a wonder that Mountain Dew actually got off the ground to become one of the most popular soft drink brands in the world today, since the Hartman brothers were so bad at marketing. Did you know that the original slogan for their product was "Yahoo Mountain Dew, it'll tickle your innards!" which, don't you agree, is cringe-worthy to say the least?

18. *Without whiskey, there would be no Tabasco™ hot sauce.* Just like a fine spirit, tabasco sauce is aged in used oak barrels that used to contain Jack Daniels whiskey.

19. *The St. Valentine's Day massacre was the result of a botched bootleg whiskey deal between Chicago mob bosses Bugs Moran and Al Capone.* The story goes, Bugs Moran, and a couple of his lieutenants were lured into a Chicago warehouse to inspect a new shipment of whiskey; what they did not know was that it was all a ploy of Al Capone to eliminate his competition. Lucky for Moran, he ran late for the meeting and escaped being included in the seven casualties of that fateful encounter.

20. *Whiskey saved the life of famous film actor Humphrey Bogart.* During the filming of his movie "African Queen" in the Congo, almost the entire crew got sick with dysentery (some of them even died because of the disease), which they contracted by drinking the local water. Humphrey Bogart was the only person spared from the ailment, because, unlike the others, he almost exclusively just drank whiskey the whole time they were there.

21. *You can turn a diabetic's urine into whiskey.* James Gilpin, a designer, researcher, and all-around weird fellow, used the urine of several elderly diabetic volunteers, which includes his own grandmother, to create a sort of high-end whiskey. Gilpin would purify the urine and, through a series of chemical processes, extract the sugar molecules from it. He would then add this sugar into grain mash to expedite the fermentation process.

22. *Jack Daniels learned the hard way that giving away branding irons with their whiskey was a very bad idea.* Jack Daniels had a unique idea to market their Old No.7 Tennessee whiskey in Australia; they included a genuine branding iron that they used for marking barrels in their "barbecue pack". In hindsight, they should have known that giving a drunk Australian man a branding iron while he is barbecuing is probably not a very bright idea. The inevitable eventually happened, in 2013, two men, were admitted to the Royal Perth Hospital with 3rd degree burns, because they thought it would be nice to have the same brand as their favorite whiskey.

23. *By an act of Congress, Bourbon has been declared as the official alcoholic spirit of the United States of America.*

24. *Whiskey was a "holy spirit".* Until the Elizabethan era, monks would actually make different spirits in monasteries, and this included whiskey. Their practice was eventually ended when Henry VIII, in a drunken rage, dissolved the monasteries.

25. *Besides Theodore Roosevelt, George Washington is probably the most badass of American presidents.* He was so badass that he actually had his own distillery in his Mount Vernon home, and by 1799, he was the largest single producer of whiskey in the United States.

26. *You can buy whiskey by the barrel.* If you are the type of person who is not easily satisfied in buying just one bottle of whiskey, then you will be pleased to know that you can visit Jack Daniels' factory, and hand-pick a barrel for you to take home. However, know that it will not come cheap, with prices starting at $10,000 per barrel, but if you do the math, buying by the barrel is cheaper. It averages to around $11 a bottle, compared to buying it retail at $25 per bottle.

27. *Bourbon whiskey got its name from the region in Kentucky that first made it, Bourbon County.* However, even if the whiskey is made anywhere else in the country, as long as it is made up of at least 51% corn, it can be labeled as bourbon. So even if the whiskey was made hundreds of miles away from Bourbon County, as long as it follows the ratio, and is still produced within the United States, it can still be labeled as bourbon.

28. *The co-founder of Alcoholics Anonymous asked for a shot of whiskey on his deathbed.* It is quite ironic that one of the founders of the hugely popular alcoholics support group AA, Bill Wilson, never lost his taste for whiskey. While on his deathbed, he told his family that he wanted to have one last taste of his favorite drink before he died, and in true AA fashion, they refused his request, which led to Wilson going under with a huge grudge against his own family.

29. *Mark Twain is a huge fan of whiskey.* Twain proved his love for aqua vitae through a quote: "Too much of anything is bad. But too much of a good whiskey is barely enough". That's the kind of thing that Tom Sawyer would say, had Twain written a book about his grown up years.

30. *The Scots brew whiskey at an outstanding pace.* It is estimated that 34 bottles of whiskey go out of Scotland every second.

31. *Whiskey straight out of distillation does not have any color, and is sometimes too sweet.* Whiskey gets its iconic amber color from the oak barrels within which it is stored. The longer the whiskey stays in the barrel, the darker its color, and more pronounced its flavor would be.

32. *The body or lightness of whiskey is mainly due to the size of the grain used in the mash.* For instance, since rye has smaller grains, rye whiskey has a fuller body than bourbon, which is made primarily from corn.

33. *It is actually a good idea to invest in a couple of bottles of whiskey.* Unlike wine that you have to store in very

careful conditions to prolong its life and drinkability, you can actually store whiskey anywhere, as long as you keep the bottle sealed up tight. Therefore, it may be a good idea to diversify your investment portfolio with a couple of bottles of good whiskey because they will surely appreciate over time.

34. *Winston Churchill drank whiskey with a splash of water for breakfast.* Another badass politician, Churchill would down his bacon and eggs with a glass of whiskey and water, and then follow it up with a nice cigar, all before commanding the British Royal Army against Nazi Germany. His fondness for whiskey may also be the reason why President Eisenhower would often dread it when Churchill came for a visit; Churchill would sometimes walk all over the White House stark naked, which bothered Eisenhower and the First Family to say the least.

35. *Whiskey actually has a couple of health benefits.* One of the most notable health benefits that whiskey has is that it contains more ellagic acid than red wine. Ellagic acid is an antioxidant that fights cancer cells and prevents them from forming in the body. Taken in moderation, whiskey can actually help prevent the formation of certain types of cancer.

Although the bits of information that you learned in this chapter may not be of much use, it is still nice to have a stock of these interesting bits of knowledge. You can dig into this list if you ever need an icebreaker, or if you want to keep the conversation going.

Chapter 5 – How to Tell if a Bottle of Whiskey is Fake

Whiskey, as previously mentioned in the earlier chapters, is not the cheapest alcoholic beverage, averaging at around $25 a bottle. This means that there will be many unscrupulous individuals, who would be more than happy to take advantage of unsuspecting folks, and sell them cheap whiskey knock offs. This chapter is dedicated to help you prevent yourself from becoming one of their victims.

The Advent of Whiskey "Fakers"

The internet made the world a whole lot smaller; it made it possible for people from across the world to communicate and trade with each other, and it became even more apparent when eBay started their operation. Thanks to eBay and other online selling platforms, it became possible for private sellers to auction their wares to a wider audience. Unfortunately, it also became the platform by which whiskey counterfeiters and cheats swindled honest people off their hard-earned money.

There are so many listings for rare and valuable bottles of whiskey and other spirits online, and not all of them offer the genuine product. If you plan on buying a bottle of vintage whiskey online, then you need to arm yourself with the right knowledge to avoid getting fleeced by counterfeiters.

Some Tips to Identify Counterfeit Whiskeys

Always ask the seller for detailed pictures of the product. Most unscrupulous sellers will upload pictures of the whiskey bottles taken from a cheap cellphone's camera, not because it is what they have, but because the grainy picture will hide the defects in the bottle that would identify it as a fake.

If you find something that you would like to buy on a website, ask the seller if he/she could provide you with more detailed pictures, and preferably close up pictures of the label. If the seller tells you that those he/she already uploaded are the best photos of the whiskey bottle, then you need to back away. If the seller can afford to buy and sell expensive whiskey, then he/she could surely afford a decent camera that can take relatively detailed pictures. This is a serious red flag so you should just cancel your plans to buy.

Only buy from sellers with 100% positive feedback. If other buyers were satisfied with the product they got from the seller, then there is a large chance that you will experience the same. Aiming for 100% positive feedback may seem a bit too much, at least 90% or 95% will do, as some people will complain if their shipment takes a bit longer than expected.

If you see a seller with a bottle of vintage whiskey priced at a competitive rate, but his/her feedback is hidden, then take that as a sign to turn around and look elsewhere.

If the deal seems too good to be true then it probably is. Another red flag you need to keep an eye out for is if the seller placed a very low price on a bottle of whiskey that usually sells for a whole lot more. Of course, the seller can say that the reason he/she is selling that particular bottle of whiskey for such a bargain is because he/she is in desperate need of money, but you should not believe that without further consideration.

Never ever buy expensive whiskey from an unknown seller. It is typically a bad idea to spend an exorbitant amount of money with a seller you do not really know. There are many legitimate private sellers online, and to find them, you just need to ask the community for recommendations (yes, there is an extensive online community of whiskey lovers), and they will give you a list of trusted sellers.

If you happen to stumble upon a new seller offering a rare bottle of whiskey at below the usual market price, then you need to be a bit skeptical. Of course, there is a distinct possibility that the new seller is honest, and the product he/she offers is genuine, but at this point, and without any positive feedback yet, you should just keep your distance.

Know what you are looking for. To become somewhat of an expert at identifying counterfeit whiskeys, you need to know what to look for when inspecting the pictures of the bottles. To do that, you need to familiarize yourself with every little detail of whiskey bottles. For instance, a 1990 Ardberg Single Malt Whiskey (valued at $230) will always have a gold capsule (the seal at the neck of the bottle). If you see bottles that have one using a different color then you can be sure that it is a fake.

The internet makes it easier to identify fakes based solely on their pictures. You just need to do a quick image search in any search engine, and you will get a plethora of pictures taken at every conceivable angle. Compare the pictures with the ones the seller provided and check for any differences.

If this is your first time stocking your whiskey collection, then just buy from your local, licensed liquor vendor. For beginners, it is generally a bad idea to buy their first bottle of whiskey online. It is better to buy in a brick-and-mortar store to make sure that you are getting the genuine product. In any case, if you do get a fake product, it is easier to report the seller to the authorities.

Caution is still your best weapon against fake whiskeys. You need to be wary and not be taken in by the sweet promises of some sellers. Do not let your eagerness to get your hands on a rare bottle of whiskey dominate your common sense.

Chapter 6 – Whiskey Cocktail Recipes

Although purists advise against drinking whiskey any other way than straight, on the rocks, or with a splash of water, beginners may find it hard to get used to its taste. The strong taste may even deter them from pursuing their hobby further. To keep things interesting, it is best to try mixing it up and use whiskey in cocktails. To get you started, here are a few cocktail recipes involving whiskey that you can try at home.

Rye Manhattan

The Manhattan is probably the most iconic cocktail that uses whiskey as its base. This recipe is for the basic Manhattan and does not require too much skill to make.

All you need to do is to combine ¼ cup of rye whiskey, a couple of dashes of bitters, and a shot of sweet vermouth in a mixing glass full of ice. Stir the contents until the outside of the glass gets cold, strain into a stemmed glass and garnish with a single Maraschino cherry.

Old Fashioned

This is the one cocktail that is almost impossible to mess up; you actually need to be a complete idiot to make a horrible Old Fashioned.

This is seriously easy to make; you just need to put a teaspoon or so of fine granulated sugar in an Old Fashioned glass (a highball glass will do if you do not have an Old Fashioned one). Put in just enough water to make a thick sugar syrup. Pour in a shot of good bourbon, and stir until everything is incorporated, then add a couple of large ice cubes and stir to chill the contents. You can garnish this with a cherry or an orange wedge if you wish.

Jack and Coke

This is the simplest whiskey cocktail recipe (I mean, the ingredients are already in the name) and despite the name, you can use any brand of soda you want.

Take 10 oz. of Coke (or you can use Pepsi, Dr.Pepper, etc.) and combine with a shot of Jack Daniel's whiskey (or any rye whiskey), mix thoroughly and throw in a couple of ice cubes and then serve. This drink is best when you just want to sit back and relax, because the soda masks most of the whiskey's strong flavors and hydrates you at the same time. Just do not drink this too often, as it will desensitize you from the taste of the actual whiskey.

Bourbon Sweet Tea

The great thing about this cocktail is that the flavors of the tea and the bourbon actually complement each other. This is also the perfect drink for those hot and lazy summer afternoons; just make a batch in advance, place in the fridge and enjoy it whenever you need a quick drink.

To make Bourbon Sweet Tea, you first need to make three cups of black tea, according to however strong you want it, pour into an appropriately sized mason jar, mix in 8 ounces of good bourbon, lemon and orange wedges, mix thoroughly, cover the jar and let it chill in the fridge before serving.

Mint Julep

This is a traditional Southern drink that will instantly perk you up, and refresh you even on the hottest of days; and what's better, is that it is actually very easy to make.

To make a simple Mint Julep, you need to place around 2 teaspoons of simple syrup and 8 to 10 fresh mint leaves at the bottom of a tall glass. Using a wooden pestle (if you do not have one, you can use the handle of a wooden spoon), slightly bruise the mint leaves (you do not need to pulverize the leaves), and then coat the sides of the glass with the mint leaves' aromatic oils. Add a half glass of crushed ice and 3 ounces of good bourbon. Mix until everything is incorporated, top the glass with more ice, insert a long straw and serve.

Whiskey Sour

The Whiskey Sour is one of the old-fashioned cocktails that has not lost even an iota of its appeal even after all these years. The tartness from the lemon juice is just enough to cut through the sometimes overpowering flavor of the whiskey; thus, making it easier to drink.

To make an old-fashioned whiskey sour, pour 2 ounces of rye whiskey, an ounce of freshly squeezed lemon juice, a teaspoon of sugar, and the white of one egg (pasteurized), into a cocktail shaker full of ice. Shake the contents for around ten seconds and strain into a serving glass garnished with an orange wedge.

The Rob Roy

Named after the iconic operetta from the early 19th century, this cocktail has become one of the most memorable drinks ever to grace this world. There are many variations of this drink that have been made throughout the years, but for most, the basic recipe is still the best.

Take 2 ounces of blended Scotch whiskey, a splash of Italian vermouth, and a dash of Angostura bitters, and place everything in a cocktail shaker with some cracked ice cubes. Shake the contents vigorously for about ten seconds and strain into a cocktail glass and garnish as you would a Manhattan.

Sea Captain's Special

This is said to be the very first cocktail to ever make use of rye whiskey. However, the stories about its origins are a bit muddled. Regardless of where it came from, it is here now, and it is delicious.

To make the Sea Captain's Special, you only need to pour 2 to 3 ounces of rye whiskey into an Old Fashioned glass with a couple of large ice chunks, followed by a dash of bitters, a dash of pastis, and top the whole thing off with sparkling white wine.

Sazerac

This is a traditional cocktail served in the French Quarter in New Orleans. Although this cocktail requires a bit more preparation, in comparison to the other recipes previously mentioned, it is still relatively easy. You do not even need to be a professional bartender to make a passable Sazerac.

First, you need to coat the sides of an Old Fashioned glass with a bit of Absinthe, fill the glass with crushed ice, and then set it aside. In a separate mixing glass with ice, combine one sugar cube, an ounce and a half of rye whiskey, and a dash of bitters; stir the contents until the whiskey and bitters are completely incorporated into each other. Take the glass you prepared earlier and discard the ice and excess absinthe, strain in the whiskey and bitters mixture into it, and garnish with a lemon peel.

Irish Coffee

Although the name plays up the stereotype that the Irish really love their booze, and in many cases they really do, this is one cocktail that you would not mind drinking on cold mornings.

In a mug, combine 6 ounces of hot black coffee, a teaspoon of brown sugar, and an ounce and a half of Irish whiskey. After you have thoroughly mixed everything, top the coffee with heavy cream and serve without stirring.

Rusty Nail

This cocktail may be a bit too strong for beginners, but it is necessary to add this recipe to this list based on the mere fact that it is an iconic drink.

Making a rusty nail cannot be any easier; you just need to pour 2 ounces of Scotch, half an ounce of Drambuie, and a dash of Angostura bitters (optional), into a whiskey glass full of ice cubes.

Whiskey Revolver

This cocktail makes use of a rye-heavy bourbon and coffee liqueur to produce something that is completely out of this world.

Take a tall mixing glass half-filled with ice cubes. Pour in 2 ounces of bourbon, half an ounce of coffee liqueur (be careful with this because it can be quite strong), and a dash of orange bitters. Stir well. Strain the contents into a chilled cocktail glass and garnish with a twist of orange (alternatively, you can flame the orange twist to release more of its flavors).

These simple whiskey cocktails are very easy to make, so whenever you want to break away from the monotony of drinking whiskey "neat" (not that there is anything wrong with that), just break out one of these recipes and whip up a simple yet refreshing cocktail.

***

Receive e-mail updates on new book releases and free book promotions from Tadio Diller. By visiting the link below

http://bit.ly/list_tadiodiller_cs

***

Conclusion

Thank you again for buying this book!

I hope this book was able to help you to gain a deeper understanding and appreciation for whiskey. Whiskey has such a deep and colorful history, which will only serve to make your entire experience drinking it better. Don't be fooled by what other people say; there is no such thing as the BEST whiskey, what only matters is whether or not you enjoy drinking a particular brand. If you did not like it, then do not doubt yourself, even though other people say that it is the best they have ever tasted.

The next step is to take the lessons you learned from this book and apply them as best as you can in your newfound hobby.

Don't limit yourself to just the contents of this book; there are literally thousands of different whiskeys out there, and you will probably not live long enough to try all of them. However, it is not too late to start and experience the wide world of whiskey as much as you can.

Whiskey is more than just a beverage, for some people it is a lifestyle.

Finally, if you enjoyed this book, then I'd like to ask you for a favor, would you be kind enough to leave a review for this book on Amazon? It'd be greatly appreciated!

Thank you and good luck!

***

Receive e-mail updates on new book releases and free book promotions from Tadio Diller. By visiting the link below

http://bit.ly/list_tadiodiller_cs

***

Check Out My Other Books

You will find these books by simply searching for them on Amazon.com

The book shows you how to make sure your next party is unforgettable. With the tips and recipes in this book you will be able to make all of your favorite cocktails right in your own home.

This book will show you everything you ever wanted to know about beer from its history to how to find the perfect beer for any meal. It will introduce you to new beers and help you explore beers beyond the common big commercial light beers.

Beer is the world's most popular alcoholic drink, but if you've only sampled the most popular brands, you are missing out some of the best tasting brews around. This book guides you to the world's best craft beers, how they are made, and what foods to pair them with.

For too many people wine can be a little intimidating. You may know you love the taste of a red or a white wine, but how do you know what kind of wine to order at a restaurant? How can you choose the right wine for your dinner party when there are so many options?

Greetings from the Lean Stone Publishing Company

We want to thank you so much for reading this book to the end. We are committed to creating life changing books in the Self Help area, such as this one that you just read.

If you liked this book and want to follow us for more information on upcoming book launches, free promotions and special offers, then follow us on Facebook and Twitter!

Sign up for e-mail updates on new releases and free promotions by visiting this link:

http://bit.ly/list_lsp_cs

Like us: **www.facebook.com/leanstonepublishing**

Follow: **@leanstonebooks**

Thank you again for reading to the end, it means the world to us!

Made in the USA
Middletown, DE
29 November 2016